SOME WHITE WALLAH

The Diary of an English Actor in India

Martin Bishop

New Generation Publishing

© Martin Bishop 2005

To Ros and Martin who stopped me from going
completely doolally.

And to Suzie for loving me enough to allow me to do it.

CONTENTS

PREFACE

On 31st May 2005 two actors, myself and Martin Aukland set out for India to take part in a production about India gaining her independence, called 1947 LIVE, written, produced, designed and directed by Aamir Husain with his wife Virat as co-director.

I was to play three roles: Sir Thomas Roe, King James 1st ambassador to the court of the Mughal Emperor Jehangir, Lord Irwin's private secretary (Lord Irwin was viceroy in 1930 at the time of the Dhandi salt march, later he was to become Lord Halifax) and finally Lord Mountbatten.

Martin Aukland was to play four roles: the Reverend Edmund Terry, friend of Sir Thomas Roe, Sergeant Terry, a police officer involved with the arrest and trial of Bhagat Singh an Indian freedom fighter who was executed by the British in 1931, Lord Irwin and Mountbatten's Chief of Staff, Lord Ismay.

Several years earlier I had spent some time travelling in the sub-continent when I my wife and I had driven from London to Bombay. During our trip we spent several weeks in Pakistan and India so I had some idea of what to expect but nothing prepared me for what was in store.

Martin and I had been cast in our roles by Ros Stockwell, an English actress with considerable experience of India. In her view our ability to cope with India was just as important as our acting credentials.

How right she was.

THE DIARY

Wednesday, 30th March 2005

I arrived at Air India and they had sent my ticket to the airport just five minutes before I arrived! Martin Aukland had already picked his up. They haven't given me an open return as I requested but we'll have to try and sort that in India. There will be a cost about £50 I think. India starts here.

Thursday, 31st March

Arrived at the airport. *"Shall I wait and see if everything is alright,"* offered Suzie.

"No, it'll be fine." Kissed and waved goodbye.

I presented myself at the Air India desk. Yes, they had the ticket. *"Passport, please."*

I opened the very neat and impressive leather passport holder only to find it empty. I stared in disbelief and then realised what I had done. Just to be on the safe side I had photocopied my passport and then … left it in photocopier. Alicia came to the rescue and raced out to me in a taxi and all was well.

On checking in I enquired as to whether Martin had checked in yet. He had, and I managed to get his seat number. I scanned the passengers in the departure lounge to look for the tall late-middle-aged actor who was going to play Lords Irwin and Ismay but there were no obvious candidates. On boarding I identified my seat and then sought out Martin. He was nothing like I imagined. Quite short, aged about 30 with a shock of dark hair. I introduced myself. He was very genial if a bit distant. I wished him a good flight and returned to my seat. The check-in girl had been a star allocating me a seat in an exit row seat with buckets of leg-room.

Friday, 1st April 2005

Arrived last night to be taken to a different hotel from the one we were expecting. No problem as it is excellent. All very five star albeit a bit anonymous.

Martin Auckland is very funny. We should work well together. I've been through all the lines with him and they seem pretty secure.

Virat and Aamir seem pleasant enough.

Very philosophical about India. Things will go wrong. At present there is a general strike of suppliers as the government is trying to introduce VAT.

Amir Hussain   Virat Hussain

Today we were taken and shown the 'stage' which is in the process of being built. The audience sit on a raised platform, which is on a turntable and moves to face the next scene. There are 15 sets in all we are told. It's rather like a huge film set: about 200 yards wide with various permanent scenes set up on three sides of the platform, the Red Fort, Jinnah's study, Jehangir's palace and so forth. Through the middle there are two parallel sets of railway lines on which complete sets are to trundle on with all the actors in place.

I enquired as to when we were opening and was told 5th April. Well I just can't see it, but then I'm new to India.

We start rehearsals tonight at about 8pm and I'm told we'll work until midnight. It could be a little chaotic. Nehru has just dropped out so they're trying to find a replacement. I expect there will be a lot of standing around, waiting for things to happen.

Martin on set

Saturday, 2nd April 2005

Went to a rehearsal last night. As expected, all very chaotic. But Martin and I did all our bits pretty well and I think we'll be alright.

Yashwant Singh who played Ghandi

The site is not far from a motorway and with the noise of that together with the construction work which goes on perhaps 24 hours a day it's hard to concentrate.

As Ros told me before I came out there doesn't seem to be any such thing as professional theatre in India but the main Indian actors we met seemed to know what they were doing. Gandhi looks a little too well-fed for my liking, but then so am I.

At first blush the directors appear to know what they want but the rehearsal process is mixed with the logistics of building the set. In the middle of a scene the director will take a mobile phone call or have an earnest conversation with one of the set builders ordering timber or paint or whatever. This is India I keep reminding myself.

We are now told the latest planned opening date is 9th April, the date having drifted four days overnight. However, I just cannot conceive that we will ready to open even by then.

The hotel is wonderful and it's a nice feeling when you are rehearsing in the dust and heat and mosquitoes of the set to know that you are coming back to unashamed luxury. I swam in the pool at 7am and then had a massage (800 rupees - £10) before breakfast.

I bought 4 litres of gin at the airport (unbelievably value – 2 litres for £15!) and asked the bell-captain to organise a case of tonic water. So I sit sipping a gin and tonic or even nicer, gin and fresh orange juice. All very civilised.

Monday, 4th April 2005

Spent yesterday afternoon around the pool. Reading and enjoying the sunshine.

One could grow very fat here. There is so much food and the coffee-shop, which is rather more than that, is open 24-hours a day. I have yoghurt and a spicy omelette for breakfast and coffee. For lunch I had chicken kebabs and peas. So I'm being careful. Bottled water. No salads. Only bananas. So far so good. Martin is not so lucky. Despite my advice, he was seduced by the salad. *"In this hotel it will be alright."* Well no, actually. So he's now laid up with serious squits and stomach cramps and has had the doctor called out to him. He will not be at rehearsals tonight.

Saturday night's rehearsal was just as chaotic. We rehearse until midnight though we spend most of the night sitting about. It's all rather more like making a film than being involved in a piece of theatre. We see little of the directors who are always occupied in a million and one other tasks. Last night I was working with Virat, the co-director. Every two minutes her mobile phone goes off and she disappears. Then she will watch a scene and say nothing. All very strange. And to cap it all I was told I was now playing a judge in addition to my other roles and was promptly given three new scenes and several pages of dialogue. Although this is India, at times it's hard not to have a sense of humour failure. In the middle of rehearsal the tailor came and measured us up for suits. Lord knows what my Thomas Rowe costume will look like. Fingers crossed.

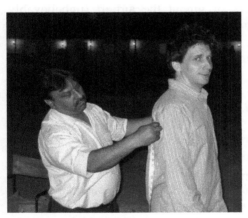

Martin being measured

When left to our own devices Martin and I work together. One day I feel he could be an excellent director and his training at Le Coq in Paris shines through. We got a fit of the giggles at a particular point and kept corpsing. We have to, to keep sane.

Today is the 4th April and I still just cannot possibly see us opening on the 9th. We haven't even got a Nehru yet! But this is India so who knows. And Virat told me that the *Wellcome Foundation* want Aamir and Virat to present a *son et lumiére* somewhere else on the evening of the 8th!

Gandhi is very good. We worked with him last night and in the absence of a director Martin directed the scene – he got real energy into his performance. Gandhi's coming over to work with us in the hotel this afternoon.

I have been told to expect a final scene but it hasn't appeared as yet. That's because it hasn't been written! But apparently it will be and it's only a page!

The other actors are very friendly and seem to hold us rather in awe. Most undeserved, at least in my case.

Tuesday, 5th April 2005

Not feeling 100% today. Nothing too serious but finding food not very interesting.

Just been to view a tomb and then went shopping with Martin. He wanted some trainers, *Converse*. He seemed to think they are rather special. After a few false starts and taxi rides we eventually found the right shop and the cost was about a quarter of the cost in the UK. So he bought three pairs.

Last night's rehearsal was much the same as before. A lot of sitting about and very little action. It's hard to get energised at rehearsal as it all seems to lack any urgency and we get precious little real direction. Also some of the other actors, Jinnah in particular, struggle desperately with lines. And we haven't seen a Nehru or a Patel yet! We open Saturday!

Martin was extremely ill yesterday and spent the day in bed being pumped full of antibiotics. He seems much better to day.

Drinking bottled water and the occasional gin & tonic. I could murder a bottle of Sauvignon Blanc but it costs a fortune in the hotel so I don't think we'll bother.

9

Friday, 8th April 2005

Heard from Suzie, in tears. Bess our one-year-old chocolate Labrador has developed a lump. Martin's brother is a vet and he asked him about Bess. His answer reads:

"Could be all sorts. And in a young dog highly unlikely to be nasty. Common things:
- *reaction to a bite or wound*
- *reaction to an injection in the last two weeks*
- *benign tumour called a hystiocytoma. Usually self resolving in a few months. Can remove.*
  After that we get onto the weird and wonderful."

So fingers crossed.

The rehearsal last night was pretty good. Most of the time we are left to ourselves. Occasionally the directors would turn up and half watch a scene and then sometimes make no comment at all. Silence. Really weird. I had a sense of humour failure when Virat started to say there wasn't enough movement in the scene without actually having seen it. And then proceeded to re-block it for the third time. But at least she appeared to have thought about it. However, when Aamir next sees it, it will probably be all changed again! The opening has now been delayed until next Wednesday. But I don't think they've realised it's the 13th and that's bad luck here. So I imagine it will be the 14th. But I finish whatever on 5th June. This evening we have off as Virat & Aamir are doing a sound and light show somewhere else! Bizarre. Still no costumes. The tailor's probably disappeared and we'll all go on in pyjamas.

Sir Sapru, classic Anglo/Indian character, more British than the British, is played by someone very Indian who has never been on stage before; in fact never worn a jacket and tie before. He doesn't seem to know quite how he should stand (he would pass muster in the defence wall for a free kick), and he is so quiet you literally cannot hear him five feet away. Bless him, it's not his fault; he is doing his best, and he has had no direction whatsoever. So in the absence of any director, Martin worked with him and I think improved his performance by leaps and bounds (at least you can hear him now) but I imagine he dreads the thought of Aamir turning up who will not recognise the moves and he will react by returning to the free kick position.

Today we actually received some of our allowance.

"Do you have our allowance?" we asked Virat.

"Do you need some."

"Yes, that would be nice."

"Tomorrow."

"But this is the third time we've been told, tomorrow."

"Oh, no."

"Oh, yes."

We received Rs5000 each within two minutes from Aamir. It really should be paid in advance. We are getting about Rs1000 or so a day which is modest enough and we are Rs3,000 behind instead of Rs7,000 ahead. By rights we should receive Rs12,000 next Monday. Fat chance, but we live in hope. I don't really want to have to ask again. All

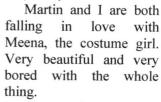

very tacky.

Martin and I are both falling in love with Meena, the costume girl. Very beautiful and very bored with the whole thing.

She spends all day and all evening there. Lummy. Last night I took her a red rose which happened to arrive on my tray for supper in my room. I delivered it with, *"Mai tum se pyar carta hu,"* which made her laugh. It means: *"I love you".* A very useful phrase. We have asked for her to be our personal dresser. Well, hello …

The border with Pakistan was opened yesterday at Srinigar. Big scenes. It's all over the press today. Families who have been separated for years meeting up. Looks like a big step forward. But the previous day the travellers' centre was burnt down by Moslem extremists. No-one was hurt except for two of the extremists who were killed.

Saturday, 9th April 2005

Received good news about Bess. Nothing to worry about.

Nothing happened yesterday. Day off. Bought a mobile phone. And found the government liquor store. The local Indian wine is quite drinkable and only Rs475 a bottle – half a day's pay - but one must get one's priorities right.

Didn't see Martin all day. I seemed to have chased him enough with ideas for doing things and he seemed a bit bored with the Red Fort. He wasn't interested in the guide who was very good. Also he really doesn't seem to want to socialise, like have a drink at the end of the day, so I just left him to it yesterday. I thought he would contact me if he wanted to. And he didn't.

Brought out a beard and a couple of moustaches for my parts as Sir Thomas Roe and Lord Ismay. Stayed in my room and tried them on. Quite remarkable how it changed my face. Spooky.

Sir Thomas Rowe

Secretary to Lord Ismay

Most of the Indian actors really seem to have very little experience, some never having been on stage before: Nehru (we now have one) is by day a forensic scientist. Gandhi however, is in a league apart. He is very good and charming. I think he could do well in the future. He gets very emotional.

It's wonderful to have the days free. So much time to do the things I've been meaning to do for years. Like write a book which is a real life treasure hunt for my children although they are now all over 25!

Thursday, 14th April 2005

Today is the opening day. Not. I have become very Indian and believed it a possibility whereas all my common sense told me that there was no way, despite the publicity posters and flyers.

Tuesday night we were called at 7pm as usual, yet didn't start rehearsing until nearly 11pm. Rehearsals went on until 3am and we eventually made it back to the hotel at 3:30am. Quite ridiculous. I hope they don't have the cast party in a brewery.

Last night we were called at 5:30pm and started by doing a bit of work and then just sat around to be finally sent home at 12:15am. I took my computer and watched a DVD - *Elizabeth*.

What seems to be lacking in India is any knowledge of or ability in project management and this is project management writ large. Having been here for a couple of weeks I still have really no idea how it is all going to work. I don't think anyone's keeping me in the dark, it's just that no-one really knows and can't deal with anything except what is immediately in front of them. Apparently there really is a final scene but as yet it still has not been written. *"Do not be worrying, it is only a page."* So I'm not worrying – if I have to walk on and read it - so be it!

And on top of it all despite all precautions, washing my hands five times a day in Dettol, I've caught some 'flu like bug. Yesterday I stuffed myself full of paracetamol. Kept forgetting my lines last night which is unlike me. Feeling a bit better today but not 100%.

Martin I think is getting a little tired of the whole thing. I suppose we just want it to get started. I predicted it would be 23rd April before the show opens. I can't really see it opening this week end so I guess it will be 21st. Maybe we will get a technical rehearsal after all. And even a dress rehearsal or are my fantasies running away with me. I am expecting us now to have to perform on Wednesdays in order to get the number of performances somewhere close to the planned 40. There really is no other way. Whatever, my last night is 5th June.

I suggested to Martin he join me on a trip and he seemed keen. But I'm learning that he's curiously difficult to pin down. I tried to agree a date to visit a tiger sanctuary and that we would hire a car and book a room at the Fort at Keroli. He insisted on two rooms which suits me but would have been prepared to share for a night to keep the cost down. All agreed. Fine. But then he changed his mind and wanted to go by train. No problem. Except not too many trains go through the tiger sanctuary.

Saturday, 16th April 2005

Still suffering with a cold. Nothing compared to poor Martin who has a rash from his knees to his neck which seems reluctant to leave. He is a great believer in alternative medicine and believes that it is a manifestation of internal torment. Wouldn't surprise me. The doctor has asked him to stop taking his malaria pills and daily vitamins (he takes several) and keep out of the sun. I suspect it's a heat rash but who knows. Let's hope he's feeling better today.

I think Aamir is a bit short of cash until the money starts rolling in. So far we have had Rs10,000 each but I don't expect to receive anything else from him until after we open. And that is now apparently Tuesday 19th. But we'll see. I sense Martin is a bit strapped and can't go out as a result. It's really not good enough.

Last night's rehearsal was the usual sitting about. Collected at 7:15pm (we always wait for up to half an hour in the lobby) only to begin work at about 10:30pm. The idea was to go though the whole things with microphones. A sort of technical rehearsal with lights and stage movement (literally - the next scene to arrive at platform 3 is the Peach Room at the Vice-Regal Lodge). There are only 8 microphones and dozens of speaking parts so one can imagine the possibilities for chaos. My first scene is as Sir Thomas Roe. I have a bucket full of lines. Martin as my chaplain has three words, *"Yes"* and *"In time"*. I have offered him some of mine but he is curiously content in his brevity. The steps to Jehangir's court have as yet to be built so we went up some side stairs which had not really been completed and were unlit and as I was climbing the stairs giving forth: *"They're touchy, these Asiatics,"* I suddenly found a step missing so the line was completed with, *"fuck me, ahh!"* The East India Company was nearly stillborn.

The rehearsal ground on (literally, not only the stages but the seating moves around with an unnerving grating and squealing between scenes) until at 2:15am, when we were just about to do my main scenes in the second half of Act 2, we were stood down.

Lord bless us and save us.

Monday, 18th April 2005

Well yesterday was a day off. A bit surprising since we were meant (once again) to open today. Not a chance. I'm told that it will now be tomorrow. Frankly I have always thought it would be 23rd which is Saturday but we'll see.

I had made arrangements to visit the New Delhi Gymkhana Club, the old British colonial club – a slice of old empire, designed by Lutyens. I called up to speak to

15

the secretary, Colonel Malhotra, and was answered by an Indian sounding voice obviously not the secretary. A conversation took place which I could overhear: *"Colonel Malhotra, there is a call for you."*

"Who is it?"

"Oh, some white wallah."

On arrival I was kept waiting for twenty minutes or so, sitting in front of the Secretary's desk whilst he went through his morning post with his PA. Odd, but this is India. I asked if I could see round the Club and a uniformed member of staff was detailed to show me round.

I first visited the Club in 1996 and as far as I could see it had changed little. The Club must have been splendid in the days of the Raj. The main rooms had echoes of grander times but are now but a sad reflection of their imperial past. There is a Rummy Room and the Lady Willington Swimming Pool – delightful colonnaded outdoor pool which must once have been the scene of languid pool parties. Lady Willingdon was the wife of the viceroy. The pool had now been roofed over with corrugated iron sheeting and the classic Roman columns around the pool painted bright blue for half their height from the top down – quite, quite bizarre. But this is India. Delightful Lutyens designed bungalows are scattered through the grounds but they seem to have seen little maintenance since independence, apart from the occasional clumsy coat of paint. Really all rather sad.

I'm going to treat tonight as a dress rehearsal and have a go at make up and so forth. Maybe I am being optimistic.

Met a friend of my wife's from England this morning and collected some goodies. Am looking forward to a decent cup off coffee, and some chocolate. A real luxury.

Feeling pretty good at the moment though I suspect my eating pattern is not good. Not enough meat and green vegetables and hardly any fruit. What am I eating? Pasta and bits and pieces.

Tuesday, 19th April 2005

I somehow thought that the night before we open might be dress rehearsal and at least for me it was going to be, so with the exception of the Sir Thomas Roe's costume from the waist down I was complete.

But what a nightmare. Nobody had told the cast and half the cast went without their costumes.

"Why are you not in fucking costume and dressed like teddy bears," called Aamir from the darkness of the seating stand.

"Nobody told us"

"We will break until you've got your fucking costumes on."

Absolute chaos.

We stopped at 2:50am and we still hadn't finished. I have only done the penultimate scene a couple of times and as for the last scene – never, as I was only given it last night.

I said at one point having had a sense of humour failure: *"This can only happen in bloody India,"* at which someone took offence. Tricky.

Will I go on pantaloon free tonight?

Martin's rash at last seems to be clearing up and he is feeling a lot better.

Thursday, 21st April 2005

Well last night we sort of opened. At least we had a preview in front of about 50 poor souls. Amazingly it went OK although Aamir didn't have a good word to say.

I thought it was a miracle since this was the very first complete run through.

You would have thought he might have given the cast a bit of encouragement. But no. He spent an hour slagging everybody off.

Tonight was another rehearsal and we open in earnest tomorrow, the 22nd, so I wasn't far out in my prediction of 23rd. Fingers crossed.

Martin now rash free.

Sunday, 24th April 2005

Well, we've had three performances if one includes the preview on the 20th. Miracle of miracles. The Times of India came tonight. I knew this because Aamir said encouragingly to the cast: *"Don't fuck up tonight, because the Times of India is here."*

Every night after the show Aamir comes backstage and slags off the cast. Yesterday was a classic. He said to some poor player, *"The dress rehearsal was fucking bad but this was even worse. Why don't you turn round and show your arse – at least we would get some expression."*

I forgot to mention that we now have a new Nehru who is extremely pleasant. I'm not sure he has done too much on stage before but at least he looks the part. He has only had a week's rehearsal and as far as I can see no intelligible direction whatsoever. He tries really hard. I worked with him tonight for about twenty minutes before the show and I felt that his confidence and his performance improved noticeably. After the show Aamir comes out with, *"Oroon (for that is the actor's name), that was the worst yet."* Jesus, he's lucky he's got any cast at all.

And despite Ros's very best advice I had a sense of humour failure three times tonight after the show.

Firstly, because we are still hugely behind in our allowance. We are each now owed Rs22,000 which is about £275. I prepared a statement and gave it to Aamir, who said he would sort it out on Monday. I realised later we aren't performing until the following Thursday and then cornered Virat and told her that it was ridiculous that we had to keep on asking for our allowance. *"Don't worry, it is not an issue."* Oh yes it is!

Secondly, without any warning or consultation I was told by Virat *en passant* that we are now performing on the Monday 9th and Wednesday 11th May. I had organised for my daughter to come out on Sunday 8th and had booked various hotels and an itinerary which is now completely shot to pieces. It seems so discourteous to make such changes without any consultation with the cast and as one can imagine I was not happy and told her so.

Thirdly, every night, despite being told we would have an air-conditioned car to take us to and from the hotel, we have to wait around after each show for at least half an hour, only to be taken back in an old 4-by-4 (no air conditioning) driven by the most lunatic driver one could possibly imagine. I was a little short again with Virat after yet again having to wait for half an hour. Tomorrow I shall organise my own transport. At least I may live to see England again.

So all in all, even for India, not a good day.

Sunday, 1st May 2005

Got to the point where I had to send a letter to Aamir setting out all my beefs in particular about the discourtesy of not telling us about the new performance dates. The money is always, *"no problem - I will give you a cheque"* – but he doesn't. What will tonight bring I wonder?

He seemed upset about the letter; said he was insulted. Frankly I can't see why – I think I've been incredibly tolerant. If anyone should be insulted – it's me. Well perhaps he should get a grip and deal with the issues instead of railing at the cast like a lunatic. The latest outburst was a classic: *"This was the worst fucking, FUCK!!! FUCK!!!!!"* rising to a frightening scream as he groped for words. Martin does a wonderful impression.

19

Onwards and upwards.

Thursday, 5th May 2005

Alicia joins me next week which I am looking forward to.

Just had lunch on the terrace at the Imperial Hotel which hints at what the Gymkhana Club might have been like. Simply beautiful art deco design which has been lovingly preserved and is superb. Sitting under an umbrella overlooking the lawn drinking a gin and tonic and eating an exquisite salad (my first in 5 weeks – I'm told all fresh food is washed in chlorine and the staff have to wash their hands every hour – so I fancied it might be safe). So far so good!

In truth much as I love India it gets wearing. Some of the worst driving that I have ever seen. And the filth and squalor: everyone just dumps everything. People sleep anywhere and you wonder at what their lives are like. The problem is so huge the mind boggles at how on earth one would tackle it given the chance.

Went to find a tiger yesterday. Martin and I caught the train to Alwar and then on to the Fort at Keroli which is simple and charming. We were upgraded to the best rooms in the place with magnificent views over the plain. I watched the misty dawn from a turret, with a bedspread wrapped around me.

Martin watching
the dawn at
Kesroli

The next day we set off early to the Tiger Reserve at Sariska. We would have liked to have gone at dawn as that is the best time to see the tigers, but apparently they were involved in a counting exercise and were not opening until 8am. I paid Rs1,200 rupees for the entrance fee and jeep hire. *"I understand you opened late this morning as you have been counting the tigers,"* I breezily offered. *"How many did you count?"*

"None. There are no tigers anymore."

Great.

Apparently last year there were 28 and now there are none. *"Poachers,"* was the explanation. Oh, yes? I'm not at all sure. There seemed precious little for any carnivore to eat. Hardly enough for a domestic cat as far as I could see. I think they just pushed off in search of fresh meat.

As we entered the reserve we met a vehicle just exiting. *"Have you seen anything?"* we enquired.

"A squirrel or two and some wild peacocks."

Later we nearly saw a leopard, apparently. But didn't.

Then on to the Sariska Palace which used to be a maharaja's hunting lodge. Lots of old photographs of maharajahs and empire builders standing proudly behind dead tigers. All a bit sad.

The guide book describes the palace as having history, location, grandeur, dirty table cloths, a dingy restaurant and no bar. Some rather sad stuffed tigers with battered whiskers stared lifelessly out of their dusty glass cages. Very depressing

A very sad looking tiger

We caught the train back and managed to get ourselves upgraded to Executive class.

Aamir gets worse. I had a blazing row with him today over dates. He had just advised Martin over the phone that we would be performing virtually every night up to the 5th June including now 10th May as well as 9th and 11th. I just happened to be there and I think the fact that the 10th had gone as well pushed me over the edge. I picked up the phone and exploded. My time with Alicia is now completely kyboshed and all because of his appalling organisation, lack of planning and abysmal communications. The problem must be that since he has managed to attract a number of sponsors he is hoist with his own petard as he now has to produce performances. Since he has lost at least 12 performances (probably a lot more since he was originally planning this for March/April) he has to make it up somehow. The thought of consulting the actors clearly didn't enter his head.

I rang Ros and asked her if she could help and she offered to ring Aamir and explain that we must have some time off.

Ros rang back later to say that she had spoken to Aamir and had agreed with him that we would after all have to have some time off. I suggested she try to agree the best deal she could but that four or five days over the next five weeks would be reasonable.

My daughter joins me on the 8th and having sorted it all out with the Lobby Manager I had been moved to a twin room so that she could stay with me. Then last night I had a call from a different Lobby Manager saying that the hotel could not allow two people to stay in a complementary room and I was asked to pay for a separate room my daughter at a cost of a mere Rs10,125 per night despite the fact that the difference between single and double occupancy is Rs500 a night which naturally I am happy to pay. It cannot be a coincidence that this has just happened. I have written a polite letter to the manager saying that there is no need for an additional room as my daughter will share a room with me and that I would be delighted to pay the difference between a single and a double room. If he does not agree my daughter will have to stay elsewhere, probably in the decayed splendour of the Gymkhana Club.

I once had a New Zealand secretary who announced that she was returning to New Zealand. A few days before she left she said: *"Four sleeps to go."*

"What?" said I.

"At Christmas as a child, didn't you count the sleeps 'til Christmas day?"

Well, I'm now counting sleeps.

Friday, 6th May 2005

Aamir has copied me an e-mail he has sent to Ros in which he says that following his conversation with Ros he was under the impression that things had been sorted out.

He then complained about all sorts of things including accusing me of ignoring him during last night's show and for later choosing to leave the set immediately at the end of the show with as he put it *"... Aukland in tow"*. He then pointed out that: *"This production has cost over £200,000 pounds and shows cannot be subservient to the visits of Bishop's family."* He went on to say: *"I have already mentioned to you that should Bishop cooperate I will **try** to get his wife free accommodation, but it all depends on him now."* I responded to him directly point by point.

When he spoke to me last night I was in the middle of preparing to go on stage and as far as I recall I responded to his greeting but I imagine not very enthusiastically. As for not staying after the show, having spoken to the cast he had announced that food was available in the reception area. Both Martin and I try to eat extremely carefully and neither of us wished to have food cooked at the site. On top of that we were both tired and we chose to go straight back to the hotel, something we would wish to do every night. If that offends him I am puzzled to understand why?

With regard to dates he originally advised me in mid March that: *"We are looking at the 3rd/4th April as the opening date. As far as the closing is concerned, I'm really not sure yet. We are looking at a minimum of 40 shows, we are performing Thurs-Sunday, we may go on to the first week of June if there's a scramble for tickets, if it's a trickle we'll close end May."* The fact that he can now sell tickets for almost every single night between now and the 5th June with additional shows on Mondays, Tuesdays and Wednesdays without any consultation with the cast leaves me speechless.

His point about the cost of the show I understand. It doesn't take a genius to appreciate that the considerable delay in getting the show into production must have caused financial problems. Had he had the courtesy to address the cast to explain the implications of the delays I imagine we could have had a sensible discussion and reached agreement on additional performances amicably. The cast could then have organised their lives around the new dates.

At the end of his e-mail he had the gall to talk about acting as a team. Aamir's idea of teamwork is him standing with the cast and crew assembled around him verbally abusing them in order to get them to do what he wants.

Saturday, 7th May 2005

Ros telephoned to say that she had agreed with Aamir that there would indeed be five days off between Thursday 5th May and the end of the run. But Martin has now been given the dates and it is actually only 2 days off, 17th/18th of May. So we do 12 shows followed by 2 nights off and a further run of 18 performances. Perhaps this is normal for India.

But we are where we are. Everything here seems to be done on the hoof. Perhaps Aamir doesn't know what he's going to do himself. Not sure planning is a strength. The worst case (I hope) is that we perform every night until 5th June. There may be days off. Or there may not.

I have now resolved for the sake of rest of the cast (not least of all Martin) to put a brave face on things and simply get through the best I can with the minimum of fuss.

My daughter arrives tomorrow and I am looking forward to spending some time with her.

Sunday, 8th May 2005

I have now come to terms with the fact that Aamir has spoilt what I had planned to be a rather special father daughter time together. Alicia now sees the sunrise on the Taj Mahal alone.

I am presently reading Mark Tully's book "The Heart of India". Plenty of Aamirs in there.

The monsoon is forecast to come early on 25th May according to *The Hindu* today.

Wednesday, 11th May 2005

Alicia is now staying at the Gymkhana Club. Last night I couldn't drum up any energy at all and delivered a performance on automatic pilot which is really not good enough. I'll have to try to summon up something from somewhere tonight.

Martin seems happy enough, especially now that at last Aamir has got the message about payment. He takes everything in his stride and tries to be jolly; the cast all seem to find him amusing. He's planning to go to Agra on the two days off and Aamir has offered to arrange a free hotel room in Agra with the ITC group which seems to point to the influence he has.

Although it would have been lovely to see the Taj Mahal with Alicia, she has gone to Agra on her own for a couple of days with a car and driver whom I have checked out. He seems to drive sensibly and is reliable. If the 17th/18th are free which still looks to be the case I shall use him to go to Jaipur. We will be staying in the Samode Haveli in Jaipur which is heavenly then on to the Neemrana Fort. Naturally I will let Aamir know.

Spent a lovely morning. Coffee at the Imperial Hotel. Best value in Delhi.

Sat in a most charming sunny atrium in a wicker chair
drinking cappuccino, eating madeleines and reading the
paper, and all for Rs141. To be recommended. Then took
a taxi south, leaving it and wandered into an area near
Humayun's tomb looking for Nizam-ud-Din's shrine.
Nizam-ud-Din is a Suffi saint. Wound my way along back
alleys wondering if I would ever find my way back and
saw a bit of life. I eventually found a rather simple
looking tomb and asked the chap there if that was it. It
wasn't, but he spoke reasonable English. He turned out to
be a book-seller from Patna. He opened up the building
for me. Inside was the tomb of a Persian poet. He
introduced me to his daughter and then offered to lead me
to Nizam-ud-Din's tomb. Off through the narrow streets
and bazaars, past flower sellers and shops offering
everything imaginable until we came to a point where we
were asked to deposit our shoes with a man in the street.
We proceeded barefoot through the narrow alleyways
emerging eventually into a sunlit busy square with the
most beautifully decorated pavilion in the middle. I was
invited in to see the tomb and pay my respects. The tomb
was strewn with flowers and offerings of silk. The walls
were exquisitely painted. Outside a harmonium was being
played with two people singing. One of those

unplannable, unmissable experiences.   Another world. Quite magical.

Thursday, 12th May 2005

Dutifully I have advised Aamir that I shall be going to Jaipur and he is happy with that. I felt like a schoolboy asking to go to the loo. He asked if I wanted help with the trip which is a step in the right direction. I have heard a rumour that there is no performance on 24th. I really don't think anyone can make any difference to what he chooses to do. He will at the end of the day do what suits Aamir.

Ros is right about this master/servant thing. The cast and crew seem like rabbits before a weasel. As he rails they just stand there transfixed. The poor driver was lambasted for some reason last night very publicly. The caste system is alive and well. As if to get his own back the driver drove like a complete lunatic with a death wish on the return journey.

Last night as I came off stage I wrote a limerick:

An Indian lawyer called Gandhi
Planned a very long salt march to Kandi
But he realised his fault
And came to a halt
And turned round and headed for Dhandi

Aamir held a warm-up before the show.   An unusual technique. The cast stood around him in a circle while Aamir spoke for 10 minutes saying something like: *"It's so fucking slow, especially the first act. It's not speed it's just picking up fucking cues. We haven't much of an audience tonight so you will have to work hard to grab them. You've got to get more fucking energy into your performance."* I felt inspired.

My performance I'm pleased to say was in fact much better last night. Martin doesn't take things too seriously

and I can't look at him during the final scene as I feel he
will corpse and me along with him. Lord Ismay was much
older than Martin and he has attempted to age himself by
pouring talcum powder all over his hair which rather
makes it look like a bouffant grey wig.

Martin's aging courtesy
of Johnson & Johnson

His suit was made by the local tailor whom I think must
have mistaken inches for centimetres and his shirt collar
seems to have a life of its own. At the end of the final
scene he crosses the stage towards me, and with collar
askew, looking by this point as if he's got a terminal case
of dandruff, and with an earnest look on his face says:
"The sub-continent may go up in flames." I daren't look
at him as I know he is about to corpse. Fortunately before I
do my move takes me to the door and I exit with: *"So be
it, Ismay. If this country wishes to tear itself apart I think
we'd better leave them to get on with it and burn in their
own hatred."* Great exit line but hard to play for laughs.

Saturday, 14th May 2005

Strange thing happened today. As I waited on the landing
the Lobby Manager with whom I had originally been

dealing came out of the lift. It was he who had organised my move to a twin room. *"Good morning Mr. Bishop,"* (I am always amazed at how these people can remember the guests' names). *"How has your daughter settled in?"* I explained the situation about which he knew nothing. Curiouser and curiouser. Having thought about it I spoke to him later and I could tell he was a bit bemused by the whole thing and offered to sort things out.

Then I met the manager's number two, Benita, in the lobby just as Alicia and I were going out of the door. I explained the problem and she too thought it was mad. She went away to check and came back and said it was the auditor who had registered the room as a single room for a foreigner with the government and it could not be changed. I wonder how the auditor picked this up? Perhaps I should have just kept quiet and not told anyone that Alicia was coming. India is such a contradiction of anarchy and red tape. So, disappointing as it is, we are where we are. Not the end of the world.

Went to visit a couple who run a guest house this morning, Avnish & Ushi Puri. Ushi is a Reiki master and is simply delightful. Her small guest house is charming and very inexpensive.

The show goes well and Alicia came last night and enjoyed it despite the first half being largely in Hindi. She sat next to a journalist from *The Sunday Times* who said she enjoyed it and when she realised that Alicia was my daughter said one or two nice things about my performance so who knows, maybe we'll get a good review. She did say however that Aamir was known for spectacle and usually the quality of the acting was very poor. Let's hope we've changed her view.

Martin, bless him, corpsed again in the last scene. During my big final speech a mobile phone rang and the chap not only took the call but walked out right in front of me chattering away. People here really are amazing. But I bravely continued to grant independence with a straight face.

Sunday, 15th May 2005

All rather uneventful. *The Sunday Times* review came out today. It begins:

"The year was 1617. The Emperor Jehangir concluded a commercial treaty with England's Sir Thomas Roe. And gradually the English took over our land and our freedom. Our minds however were still liberated. And slowly but surely pockets of people around India began to rise against the atrocities of the British."

So, not popular then. Were we really that bad? But I don't suppose for us English the Norman French were at the top of everyone's Christmas card list!

There really are one or two good performances in particular Yashwant Singh as Gandhi and Jaspir Malik as Jinnah.

Yashwant Singh as Gandhi   Jaspar Malik who played Jinnah

My daughter and I both agree with the press about the performance of Jinnah. Jaspir Malik is absolutely charming and is perfectly cast. He is now in his mid-seventies and has wonderful presence both on and off stage. To see him and Yashwant Singh on stage together is to quote *The Sunday Times*, *"a pleasure to watch"* and they were rightly praised.

The review managed to mix up Martin and myself (not surprising since they got us mixed up in the programme – too many Martins) but describes the performance as Mountbatten as *"compelling"* which is encouraging.

Two days off on Tuesday. Off to Jaipur and the Neemrana Fort. Then 18 shows on the trot. Phew!

On, on, on, on, on.

Monday, 16th May 2005

Another sponsored performance last night.

Act 2 opens with a scene between Martin as Lord Irwin and me as his secretary. The scene ends with Martin quoting from a letter which Gandhi has written to him about his intentions to break the salt law by marching to the sea to make salt. Martin concludes the scene with the words: *"If he wants to march, let him march."* Long before he's got to this point the motor driving the seating platform whirs into life and the platform begins its grinding, squealing way round to face the next scene, the Dhandi salt march. Rather distracting. Each night the motor strikes up earlier and earlier much to Martin's and my amusement. As the motor grunts into life I have now introduced a little cough which Martin acknowledged last night with a small cough of his own. A truly great theatrical moment.

Tuesday, 17th May 2005

Hired a car and a driver and drove down to Jaipur. The driver was sullen but I had used him before and he drives safely even if despite my best efforts he seems congenitally unable to smile. He had a disturbing habit of letting out a loud belch from time to time. I inwardly groaned. We stopped on the way for a tour of the Amber Fort and an elephant ride only to be pestered and pestered

32

by traders trying to sell craft ware. I eventually came out with, *"What is it about the word 'no' that you don't understand?"* It amused some tourists but was rather lost on the trinket salesman.

We checked into the Samode Haveli which is simply delightful. Much better in my view than the swish places like the Rambargh Palace. The room was amazing. Called the *shish mahal* which I think means mirror room. It's all original and the walls and ceiling are covered with tiny convex mirrors which reflect the light of a candle like a thousand twinkling stars.

My daughter treated me to a massage. All very sensual: being totally naked and covered in hot oil with an Indian evening raga playing in the background. Sadly the masseur was not a sweet Indian maiden but a charming young man but he was extremely good. Then into the hottest steam room I have ever been in. I had to cover my face to breath and eventually gave up, grabbing for the door.

Wednesday, 18th May 2005

Tour of the City Palace with a wonderful guide who spoke perfect English and knew his stuff. One maharaja of Jaipur, fairly recent, was enormous standing 6'6" tall and almost as broad weighing in at 250kg. He had 108 wives. One has to feel for them.

Then off to the Neemrana Fort in the baking afternoon heat. Potentially a wonderful place to stay but in the blistering heat it rather fell short of the mark.

The pool which in the brochure is an exquisite blue had turned a sort of luminous green. *"But the pool is green,"* I observed to the young Indian showing me round.

"Yes, there is a colour fault."

The place is noted as a health spa and apparently offers Kerula type treatments. There were treatments for nervous weakness, stress and strain, emaciation, for proper brain functioning, obesity, nose cleansing, urinary tract infection, ear wax and so on. The treatment usually involved having hot oil or ghee poured into one orifice or another, including ears, nose, mouth and all places south.

One in particular I felt no difficulty in avoiding was *Vasthi: for proper peristalis* which involved *"certain oils, herbal extracts etc being applied through the rectum for a period of 7-21 days"*. Perhaps not surprisingly it held itself out as an effective treatment for constipation.

Thursday, 19th May 2005

Drove back to Delhi and said goodbye to Alicia at the airport. It has been wonderful to spend some time with my daughter. The first time just the two of us have been together for any period as far as I recall.

During my travels I started to read Patrick French's *Liberty or Death* which is a wonderful read about the independence of India. He is so objective about the people and events. But I suddenly found myself reading some of my lines from the play as Lord Irwin's secretary which had obviously been lifted word for word from the book. The script had clearly been copy-typed from a badly handwritten draft and some words were missing or obviously mistyped. I was able to fill in the missing words and correct some of my speeches, so tonight performance will be a little different.

At the moment they seem to be rebuilding the hotel and there's a thump, thump, bang, bang, going on all the time. I'm just glad I haven't got a headache but at this rate perhaps I soon will have.

Ros e-mailed me to say she was going back into acting. *"Middle aged woman, young at heart, seeks acting work, and part time theatre studies teaching."* Awfully brave of her. I'm full of admiration. I have a feeling that she will do very well. I once went to a lecture at the Royal Geographical Society given by Reinhold Messner who is perhaps the world's greatest climber. Amongst other feats he is the only man to climb Everest truly alone with no oxygen and the north face of the Eiger, again alone, taking about 10 hours when everyone else takes two to three days. At the conclusion of his talk he said in his strong

German accent: *"At the end of your life, it is not what you have that matters: it is what you have done."* He received one of the longest standing ovations I have heard at the RGS.

Friday, 20 May 2005

Last night's performance went off without a hitch … all except for Martin losing his voice. He has been directed in his scenes as Sergeant Terry to speak in a way that relies heavily on techniques perfected at the Brian Blessed school of acting: **"LIES. THEN IT'S HIS WORD AGAINST MINE!"** I think having two days off must have seduced his vocal chords into thinking their torment was over and they simply weren't prepared for it all to start up again. He played his final scenes as Lord Irwin and Lord Ismay in a sort of hoarse whisper. *"India … may … go … up … in … flames,"* he gasped across the stage, his voice having almost completely disappeared. Let's hope it improves today.

Since I have accepted now that we will never be consulted or informed about dates, after the show last night I idly inquired of the Assistant director if there were any news on the remaining performances. The response was: *"We're selling tickets for all dates. If sales don't go too well we may have a day off."* How generous.

I find myself praying for rain. One of the actors, Oroon, who plays Nehru, has been asked by the BBC to act as casting director for the Indian actors for Freedom at Midnight. He thought he had to cast just one or two Indian parts but has been given a long list including some English parts including Lord and Lady Mountbatten. Would love to have a go for Mountbatten but I'm really not physically like him enough – too old and too much around the waist! And in truth I don't really look like him very much. Apart from that I'm perfect. But either the part of Lord Ismay or Sir Cyril Radcliff would do very nicely. Lord Ismay's left hand was missing. I think I can manage one-handed acting very well, some might say a strength. Martin tried for a while to play Ismay with one hand. He contrived this by hiding his left hand in his shirt and sort of pulling it up into his sleeve. This had the effect of raising his shoulder and distorting his jacket and he gave a commendable impression of Richard III. In the interests of art, if not truth, Ismay now has two hands.

Martin
the one
handed
actor

Saturday, 21 May 2005

Well last night's performance was awful.

The day began with Martin and I having breakfast. His voice was little better and did seem to improve to some extent over breakfast so we were optimistic that it may recover as quickly as it had collapsed. Later, Martin consulted the doctor who naturally advised him to rest his voice and not perform that evening.

We met again later in the afternoon and it was obvious his voice had deteriorated badly and that he sensibly should not perform. We worked out contingency plans. I would take his mike during the Sergeant Terry scenes and he would mime to my voice. Not wonderful but better than nothing. In Act 2, Scene 1 we would reverse roles, with me taking over as Lord Irwin. We would combine

Irwin's speeches with the secretary's into a sort of monologue for Lord Irwin with the occasional grunt from the secretary. It would also have the benefit of establishing me for Scene 2 which I would do from the book. The final scene between Lord Mountbatten and Lord Irwin would be condensed to avoid Martin having to speak apart from the occasional acknowledgement. All very sensible. Not perfect but with no understudy or contingency plans there was little option. But it was not to be. Martin duly reported to Aamir who said that Martin should have told him earlier. Well he had done, the night before. And so had I. His advice at that time was drink honey and lemon. He then decided that we should proceed as usual with Martin doing the best he could. Quite ridiculous. But Martin agreed despite the doctor's good advice. By the end of the evening his voice had completely had it and he was barely audible. Apart from anything else it wasn't fair to the audience.

I have to say I was very angry about the whole thing which I thought preposterous and the anger was channelled into my performance as the rather unpleasant English judge who took on a rather terrifying persona for the evening.

Having changed after the show as usual we went to the reception area to await our lift back to the hotel where we witnessed the most dreadful of scenes. Aamir was stood in the middle of a group of the cast and crew railing like a madman at one of the cast. Aamir then actually hit him. He then called forward our driver and railed at him and then struck him too. A third was called forward who approached like a lamb to the slaughter and the railing continued. Lord knows what it was all about but I have to say I was seriously thinking about stepping in. It was a primitive, very public display of brute power. Aamir's style of teamwork writ large. Martin, who is a gentle, loving person, was extremely upset.

He said he was ready to get on the next plane. Perhaps with his voice the way it is he should do just that.

Before we left Martin again spoke to Aamir about his voice. Aamir apparently said that what we needed was a miracle and suggested that a series of acupuncture treatments would cure the problem. He asked him to come to his room at the hotel after the show.

Following the incident our driver was not unnaturally sullen and silent. Yet as we waited in the car to leave, he suddenly exploded at one of the cast through the window of the vehicle in a most vicious manner. I was expecting a wild ride back to the hotel but he actually drove quietly for a change. Thank heaven for small mercies.

Martin duly contacted Aamir at about midnight and was told to come back at 10:30 in the morning, again which he did. Virat answered and it was obvious she had just woken up, so we are no further forward. Martin is now off to the hospital to see the ENT specialist. The advice is bound to be to rest his voice. He must realise that his voice is his livelihood and if he goes on like this he could damage it permanently. I wait with interest to see how it all works out. I wonder if Aamir will have the courtesy to contact me if I am expected to step in or will he just pass a message down via the cast. Nothing now would surprise me.

Sunday, 22 May 2005

Last night's performance was no better. Despite the advice from the ENT specialist Martin again agreed to perform. By the end of the evening he was again barely audible and to give the audience a chance of understanding what was going on I had to repeat part of his lines so that things would at least make some sense. Aamir had organised an acupuncture session during the day but Martin had to pick up the fairly sizable bill which didn't please him too much. He said he felt no better after it, if anything a bit worse.

But finally after the show Aamir agreed to stand him down tomorrow. Apparently he is getting a stand-in from somewhere. I told them that I was available all day to work with the stand-in but all I was asked to do was to be at the site at 6:30 instead of 7:00. But this is India: it won't be 6:30 it will be at least half an hour late so we will go on with no preparation whatsoever.

Monday, 23 May 2005

A quiet day. By 5pm I had received no call so on my own initiative I decided to turn up early. On arriving I found Virat rehearsing in the site office with the stand-in, Imran. He is very young and good looking and presently has a couple of roles on television. He had a good clear voice and spoke English well. He had obviously been working hard on the lines but there is no way in my view that anyone can learn and retain that many lines that quickly with almost no rehearsal on stage, but Virat insisted that he go on without the book and with no special announcement.

Imran was very good to work with and despite the lack of rehearsal we managed to get a surprising amount out of our scenes together. As far as words go he did pretty well but the final scene turned into one long monologue for me as Imran completely blanked. He was so apologetic afterwards but it was hardly his fault. I thought he did amazingly well.

Afterwards all Aamir could say was, *"You must pick up your cues quicker."* I don't think I have ever heard him say a nice thing about anyone's performance. Is this an Indian thing? Would he somehow lose face by doing that? How he gets actors to work for him is a complete mystery.

I met Martin at breakfast this morning and exchanged a few signs with him as he has sensibly taken a vow of silence. I thought he looked tired and drawn. We now communicate by text message.

What is it about India and time? No-one, not even intelligent people, seem to have any concept of time which endlessly leads them to make impossible promises which they must know they cannot keep. Are they uncomfortable about facing up to reality, preferring to tell you want they think you will want to hear rather that anything that remotely resembles truth? Their politicians must be a nightmare. In the reception area for the show there is a coffee stand producing cappuccinos and espressos. I ordered a coffee and was told that the machine was not ready and I would have to wait three minutes. I waited for a minute or so and then realised the machine had not even been switched on let alone boiled the water. It was obvious to anyone with half a brain cell that it would be at least half an hour before there would be any coffee. I put it to the charming young man who spoke good English that his three minutes was highly optimistic and that rather than wait I may as well come back later. He quickly changed his estimate to 20 minutes. I finally got a coffee an hour later.

Tuesday, 24 May 2005

Imran stood in again last night. He really is very good. I turned up early again and managed to get a bit of time with him and he seemed pretty secure on his lines. It all went fairly well until the scene between Ismay and Mountbatten when a key cue didn't come. I had to rapidly rewrite my lines and deliver them at the same time and managed to mix up two speeches. Somehow I got out of it but it was a real tightrope wobble.

Today is a rare thing. A day off. What to do...? What to do ...? The other day before Martin became a mute we went to the railway museum. A young man showed us round various viceroy's and maharaja's carriages. Sadly they were all falling apart but one could still detect echoes of former grandeur. For artistic verisimilitude there were a number of manikins in careless poses dressed variously as The Prince of Wales in 1890 (very dapper in a neat single breasted suit and a small red bow tie) and a maharaja or two. The young man insisted on putting a maharaja's turban on Martin who rather objected as it was rather small and very scratchy. I have photograph of him looking very glum.

I was meeting the BBC tomorrow morning at 9pm but it's just been cancelled. Let's hope it's merely postponed. Apparently *Freedom at Midnight* is a semi-documentary. Maybe I can make a pitch for the voice-over.

I was also asked last night if I wanted to be put forward for an Indian movie. Well. Who knows? I could be the love interest: young Indian beauty falls for older English gentleman. Perfect story line for Bollywood. And dance? My step-ball-change is a wonder to behold.

Ros quotes an Indian friend of hers as referring to rubber time. Seems to sum it up perfectly. But when you come from a culture where being on time is so important it is so frustrating. When given a period of time I now enquire for instance, *"Is this an Indian ten minutes or English ten minutes."* It usually raises a smile and elicits a more truthful response. So I am making progress I feel. To illustrate my point, when I went to the coffee stall last night I was told, *"The coffee will be two minutes, and tonight I am telling the truth."* And he was. And he makes the best coffee in India.

Wednesday, 25 May 2005

Yesterday: a day of rest. And I did very little. Just too hot. I had plans to go to the sound and light show at the Red Fort in the evening but for all the willing spirit, the flesh was weak. Spent most of the day reading Patrick French's *Liberty or Death* and kept coming across more and more lines which made it into the play. The Express today quotes Virat as saying that they spent *'three or four months researching it.'*

All still quiet on the Martin front. Literally. And he seems to have totally withdrawn into self-imposed purdah. Perhaps he will emerge like a beautiful butterfly from the chrysalis of his silent world. Perhaps his voice will have been magically transformed as in some feel good fifties movie and he will now speak like Richard Burton:

"To begin at the beginning: It is spring, moonless night in the small town, starless and bible-black, the cobblestreets silent and the hunched, courters'-and-rabbits' wood limping invisible down to the sloeblack, slow, black, crowblack, fishingboat-bobbing sea."

Off now for Reiki treatment – a first.

Thursday, 26 May 2005

Yesterday Sunil Dutt, the actor-politician died. The newspapers are full of little else. He was plainly hugely popular and not just through his fame as an actor. For a politician to be described as a "good man" is surely a rare thing. One of his last acts was to send Rs25,000 to the widow of a labourer who had donated his organs to save six other lives. The show last night was to have been for the military but with the death of Sunil Dutt they could not attend and the show was cancelled.

Well, Martin emerged blinking into the sunlight, pumped up his wings and spoke. A voice certainly, but nowhere near a full recovery. He really should rest for a week. He confessed to me that whereas he would normally be eager to get back to the show in this case he really couldn't summon up any enthusiasm. I know how he feels. It is so unrewarding. There is no curtain call and no-one ever gives encouragement or feed back. I try really hard with Nehru, Gandhi and Jinnah to praise their performances which I hope helps. But I suspect like me they are counting the days.

Martin found himself in the hotel lobby yesterday when Bill Clinton arrived. Martin seems to idolise him. Bill Clinton shook everyone's hands including Martin's. He moved on and then came back and shook Martin's hand again. Sadly Martin's camera had almost run out of power and all he got was a photograph of the back of Bill Clinton's silvery head before his camera completely died.

He later bought Bill Clinton's autobiography and was tipped off as to the room where he was staying. Bold as brass he went up and knocked on the door and asked the secret service man if Bill Clinton could sign his book. Sadly it wasn't possible but top marks for trying.

Since the show was cancelled I suggested that Martin and I go to the *son et lumiére* at the Red Fort. Martin decided not to go so I went alone as it is likely to be the last opportunity I would have. It really is very good and the sound system, which is excellent, is all around you. The show essentially tells the history of the Red Fort through the history of the moguls. It describes them as descending from Genghis Khan which is not really true. Babur was the grandson of Timurlane who was one of the most murderous individuals that ever lived (he is now worshipped as a hero in Uzbekistan). His practice was to build towers of heads around conquered cities. When he sacked Delhi he killed practically everyone and the city took 100 years to recover. The story as told eulogises the freedom-loving Indian but I have to say rather looks at history through rose tinted Indian spectacles: perhaps unsurprisingly the atrocities committed by the Indians during the 1857 Sepoy mutiny, particularly the episode where the English women and children were butchered by the King's servants under the *Pipul* tree in the Red Fort, did not merit a mention.

The Reiki treatment yesterday was fascinating. Ushi and I spent half an hour or so before the session talking about Reiki. I have to say I had some difficulty in grasping it all but it seems to be about channelling the life force, the soul, I suppose. She then lit some incense and drew the curtains and I lay on the bed face up with my eyes closed. She didn't touch me but I could sense her presence and the light occasionally darkened as she must have passed her hand over my face. After a while I became conscious of my hands and feet tingling, gently throbbing even. I soon fell into a delicious sleep. When I awoke she was gone and at least an hour had slipped away.

I just lay there for a while as I felt such an intense sense of calm.

Afterwards we discussed the experience. She said that she felt a lot of energy being put into organising my life but then at one point, for about four minutes she said, she felt me saying that I just wanted to be me. And then it all became fuzzy again as if it was being painted over. I have to say I felt very calm; I still do.

Friday, 27 May 2005

Yesterday was another quiet day. I received a phone call at about lunchtime to say the show had again been cancelled. No reason given. So yet another, a third, night off.

Martin had been offered a car for the day by the bell captain and we planned to visit all seven Delhi cities. But in the end a car wasn't forthcoming and so I spent the afternoon reading.

In the evening in the pursuit of the Bill Clinton deity we decided to splash out and dine in Bukhara, one of Bill C's favourite restaurants, which is described as being world famous and the 14th best restaurant in the world. We arrived at 8pm and were placed on a table for two, a good position close to the door so Martin could perhaps meet his hero again. The Bukhara is famous as a kebab house and for its dal. Martin wanted to eat a vegetarian thali which we decided to share to keep the cost down. (It's a bit like going to an Argentinean restaurant and saying you don't want to eat steak). The dal came in a small dish with a skin on it like school gravy which we stirred in. The vegetarian food was distinctly ordinary and it's hard to see what all the fuss is about. Perhaps the kebabs are exquisite. To cap it all, a no-show from the big C.

Having had the vegetarian thali we decided to move to the Coffee Shop for pudding and try the Kulfi. Very dangerous and something I have avoided like the plague.

It arrived, yellow, on a bed of gelatinous white vermicelli with a dribble of red sauce over it. Martin didn't touch his. I separated the kulfi from the vermicelli and scraped off the red dribble. Strange taste. Not really like ice-cream. A bit like rather soft iced nougat with bits of pistachio in it.

The head chef was passing and we engaged him in conversation. He told us how the Bukhara had not changed its menu in 14 years. And it clearly doesn't need to as it was full. We shared with him how at the hotel sadly we felt compelled to avoid the salad which is something we had missed. He then proudly told us that this was the only hotel in India with a particular health certificate and how British Airways had tested the food for hygiene and scored it 98%. We could eat anything. So who knows: tomorrow a crisp salad niçoise?

Saturday, 28 May 2005

Will I never learn. Last night I was so ill. I think I must have eaten from the 2% British Airways missed. My guts churned and groaned. In the morning I began to wretch violently but brought nothing up. I felt simply dreadful. I took two Ciprofloxacin and withdrew from the world. Food lost all it's appeal and I spent the day fasting. Sadly the show wasn't cancelled and Imran was by now playing another part as one of the Indian actors had had a bereavement. So like an old trouper I emerged from my Cimmerian darkness and prepared for the evening's performance.

Martin's voice had benefited from another night off and he treated it with respect giving a much more *sotto voce* Sergeant Terry.

The start of the second act was bizarre. Martin and I took our positions as Lord Irwin and his secretary on the unlit set as usual where we engage in quiet conversation until the lights come up and we begin our dialogue.

Secretary to
Lord Irwin

We waited … and waited … and waited. Eventually there
was an announcement:

"Please return to your original seats." We'd had this
before. Pause.

"Please return to your original seats," a little more
forcibly.

***"WOULD EVERYONE PLEASE RETURN TO
YOUR ORIGINAL SEATS OR YOU WILL BE
CHARGED THE DIFFERENCE."***

Then unbelievably a checking process commenced.
There was a great kafuffle and it was like some mad party
game of musical chairs. I have never seen anything like it
in the theatre. The audience were none too pleased and
after a while ripples of applause broke out which I learnt
afterwards was meant to encourage us to start. And then
suddenly the lights came up and we started.

In preparation for coming out here I had bought a beard
and moustache for the Thomas Roe part together with a
couple of moustaches for the other roles. As Martin had
none and I had one to spare I offered him one for his role
as Lord Irwin. Instead of putting it carefully away after
use each night he simply placed it in his top pocket which
seemed to work well enough. Having had three days off
and with someone else using his costume perhaps
unsurprisingly it had disappeared. Instead of getting the
make-up people to make up one for him (and they are very
good) he went on without one. To quote Martin: *"I*

thought about it for a moment and then thought: well ...."
The only discernable difference now between Lords Irwin
and Ismay is the suit and the grey hair, courtesy of
Johnson & Johnson.

Sunday, 29 May 2005

Last night began with Martin being quite morose to the
point where I just gave up trying to have any conversation
with him. He apologised later and said that he had just had
it. He felt the time off for his throat followed by a further
three days off when there was no show just finished him.
Mentally he seemed to be willing himself back home in
Paris.

Martin quickly changed into his
costume as the Reverend Edmund
Terry. His costume, incidentally,
is a sort of long black cloak affair
with a large black velvet four
cornered hat which he has to wear
diagonally as it's the only way it
will fit. Alicia thought he looked
rather like more like a
highwayman than a clergyman
and dared me to refer him as the
Reverend Richard Turpin as
opposed the Reverend Edmund
Terry. I have to say my courage failed me.

Having changed, he promptly disappeared. I enquired
of the assistant director at to what the plans were for the
next week to be told that Monday, Tuesday, Wednesday
and Thursday were all cancelled and that Friday is to be
the last night. I quickly made my way to the set where I
suspected Martin had escaped to and sure enough found
him there lost in his thoughts. I broke the news to him.
One could see his spirits lift visibly. Personally, I still
can't quite take it in.

So we're now demob happy. Last night's performance was much as usual and I have to confess that Martin and I are both now hopeless cases having reached the hysterical stage. We simply can't act together anymore without corpsing. Last night I had to bite my knuckle nearly to the bone whilst Martin very earnestly read a letter from Gandhi. And each night when Patel says: *"I agree,"* in the penultimate scene, I just know Martin, who fortunately is upstage of me at this point, is a goner.

Patel complete with bald wig

Martin and I spent a couple of hours today looking at video clips we made in the early days. You can see the initial enthusiasm gradually decline into cynicism until we eventually obviously just hit the wall and the videos cease.

Suzie joins me tomorrow. It will be a bit strange since we have never been apart so long in 33 years of marriage.

Monday, 30 May 2005

A good performance last night.

For the past several weeks almost every night, after debating the question at some length with Nehru, Jinnah and Gandhi, I have reluctantly agreed to the division of India. I have a scene with Gandhi where he pleads with me not to divide India. It is powerfully written and I suspect based on Gandhi's own words. It moves the audience, some of them to tears I'm told, and almost always gets a strong round of applause at the end of the scene which Yashwant Singh as Gandhi richly deserves.

In the final scene, which must be an emotional experience for the Indian audience, I talk about the loss of control and the British leaving India to burn in their own hatred. It was brought home to me the other night by a lovely man in his eighties who sought me out to say how much he enjoyed the performance. He went on to tell me that in 1947 as a Hindu he had fled Lahore leaving with only the shirt on his back. He lost everything except his life. It is frightening to think that over a million died in the carnage that followed independence. But from what I have read I remain unconvinced that it could have been avoided by not dividing India. Had it not been done I wonder whether we would now be blaming the carnage on the failure to recognise Pakistan as a separate nation.

In preparing for the role of Mountbatten it was necessary for me to try to understand in some small measure the difficulties, in particular what is often referred to as the communal violence, which eventually led to partition. One thing that has struck me both from the written sources and from the play itself is the use of this word 'communal'. Indeed a letter to *The Times of India* today uses the word communalism. Nehru himself once complained, *'Many a congressman was a communalist under his nationalist cloak,'* although perhaps a little unfairly in 1947 LIVE this line is given to Jinnah. What particularly struck me was that the word seems to be used in quite a different way in India from how the English would naturally use it. Firstly, it is pronounced differently with the accent in India being in the first syllable, cómmunal, where as in England it is on the second syllable, commúnal. For me as an Englishman it is used, for example, where a group of people do something together such as participate in commúnal prayers, or jointly own something like a commúnal village hall. But in India it seems to have a quite different meaning, almost the opposite, meaning in fact sectarian, or simply racist. Being cómmunal in India would seem to be merely a euphemism for racial prejudice.

There are now far more people living in Britain whose origins lie in the sub-continent than there ever were British living in India. Whereas it would be foolish to say that division and racial prejudice does not exist in Britain today it is fair to say that our politicians and society at large work hard in trying to ensure that all communities are valued for the contribution they make to our way of life within our multi-ethnic, multi-racial, multi-cultural, multi-religious, post-colonial Britain.

I treated myself to a massage again today. It was explained to me that there were two types: the first was from the neck down and the second, the Indian massage, involved two masseurs and covered the whole body. I took the plunge. First I was ushered into the steam room and was put on gas mark 5 for ten minutes. The two masseurs then led me to the massage room. I had brought my computer on which I had copied my Indian Ragas and set it away playing. The first track was for the voice and one of the masseurs immediately recognised the artist and started to quietly join in. The lights were lowered and I was then asked to lie completely naked face up and the massage began with the two masseurs working in tandem, each taking one side starting at the foot and going all the way up to my head and back again. I had to say I found it difficult to relax feeling rather vulnerable but in the end I just gave in to the music and the gentle rhythms and drifted away.

Aamir's up to his tricks again. He seemed to have overlooked signing my cheque, on the front this time and Martin's had the account number missing. I've tried to ring him but can't get through so I left a text message and managed to contact the assistant director who tells me that he is seeing Aamir later and will bring me a new cheque. I rather doubt it.

We are not performing Monday, Tuesday Wednesday or Thursday this week and I am told that Friday will be the last night; but what an audience: The Prime Minister and Sonia Gandhi, the chairman of the Congress Party.

Suzie arrives this evening.

Tuesday, 31 May 2005

Last night before Suzie arrived Oroon rang and asked if I would like to visit Dilli Haat which is a craft market. It is rather different for Delhi and provides an outlet for real craftsmen from all over India. There was a lovely atmosphere and very little pressure to buy and prices were reasonable. No bargaining worth speaking of which was joy. I bought a silk scarf and a carved camel bone paper knife and some exquisite little hand painted tiles in a strong Persian blue to use as coasters. They cost Rs10 each. After this I headed off for the airport.

Suzie arrived an hour or so late and it was wonderful to see her after all this time. She looked radiant and full of life.

We have just had breakfast round the pool. In many ways it is the best time of the day. Cool in the shade with a gentle breeze wafting around. Today we shall see a bit of Delhi, perhaps Humayun's tomb followed by a light lunch at The Imperial.

Wednesday, 1 June 2005

Last night Oroon took us to the Lodi Gardens where the ruins were lit up. A really good time to see it. A place for lovers. And then on to a rooftop restaurant overlooking some other illuminated ruins, a place which no tourist would easily find.

Oroon who eventually played Nehru and his wife with Suzie and me at a restaurant near the Lodi gardens

Following a leisurely breakfast this morning we met our driver who was clearly not very well. We travelled to Agra with our driver sneezing and snivelling away and if one of us doesn't catch something it will be a minor miracle. We stopped on the way to view the tomb of Akbar the Great. Before dinner we paid a visit to the Taj Mahal but viewed from the other side of the river and watched the sun set where we encountered a rather colourful individual.

I imagine when the river is full in the winter the reflections must be wonderful. We sat on the edge of the foundations which Shahjahan had laid for his own mausoleum. It was to have been a mirror image of the Taj Mahal but in black marble. Sadly, his son Aurangzeb usurped the throne, murdering his three older brothers, who are incidentally buried at Humayun's tomb, and imprisoned Shahjahan in the Red Fort at Agra. So it was never built. He was buried in the Taj Mahal rather uncomfortably out of symmetry alongside his wife Arjumand Banu Begam, better known as Mumtaz Mahal.

Thursday, 2 June 2005

We got up very early at 5am to visit the Taj Mahal to watch the sunrise. By the time we got going the sun had already risen, probably at about 5:20. We eventually arrived at the Taj at about 5:40 to find that it did not open until 6am. A local found us, as they do, and took us off to the top of a local hotel which was an excellent viewing point.

We entered at 6am: there was hardly anyone there. Quite magical and took hundreds of photographs including the "Diana" shot on the bench. Although we had seen it before we still both found it simply breath-taking.

We had planned to go to Fetehpur Sikri but came to the conclusion that it would be far too hot so instead went to find Itimad-ud-Daulah's Tomb which is on the east bank of the Yamuna to the north of the Taj Mahal. Itimad-ud-Daulah was the treasurer to the Mughal Empire and the father of Nur Jahan, Jehangir's favourite wife.

The building is simply exquisite and described as a jewel box in marble. It was completed just three years before the Taj Mahal was begun and it must have had a huge influence on its design. There is extensive use of *petra dura* but the stones tend to be yellows and greys and with the white marble from a distance it gives the impression of carved ivory. We were almost the only tourists there and it is amazing that it is not on the tourist trail.

Itimad-ud-Daulah's Tomb

We drove back to Delhi with our driver in very poor shape. He looked simply dreadful and I felt sure he was beginning to fall asleep so I kept talking to him. We went through a dust storm through which it was impossible to see much and then through pouring rain. So strange weather indeed.

On the way back I received a text to say that now we are now performing on both Saturday and Sunday. Fair enough. Still no news about the cheque.

We had supper in the room.

Friday, 3 June 2005

Suzie is not well. She had an awful night. She has been sick and has the squits. She is incredibly stubborn and is reluctant to take anything despite the fact that Alicia recommends 2 x 250mg of ciprofloxacin. After much cajoling she eventually took two. A short time later she was sick and thinks she threw one back up. I persuaded her to take another and she eventually took one more, or rather half a 500mg tablet. We have now called the doctor. So much for the chef and his health certificate. That's everyone now who has got ill in this hotel, Martin, Alicia, myself and now Suzie. It's just an occupational hazard I'm afraid in India.

I have just checked my e-mail to find I have left our passports in the Trident Hotel in Agra! They are going to courier them to us.

Saturday, 4 June 2005

Suzie developed a temperature and seemed in a bad way so we got the doctor out. He was very good and prescribed a few things for the nausea, the temperature, the dehydration and the squits. This morning she seems a lot better.

Last night's show was uneventful. The Prime Minister and Sonia Gandhi did not attend but the Chief Minister for Delhi, who rejoices in the name of Mrs Sheela Dikshit, attended in their place.

The set is getting very shaky as we limp towards the end of the run. Attention to detail, not ever much in evidence, is slipping. As I sat waiting for the Vice-Regal drawing room to trundle into position I noticed a picture hanging askew. I attempted to straighten it but had not the courage to do the job properly in case it collapsed altogether, and it slipped back to its drunken angle. I then noticed the two table lamps which looked as though they had survived the siege at Lucknow. They were both bent at a curious angle and had been patched up with blue electrical tape. I inwardly sighed.

On the Irwin set there is the viceroy's desk: a small black table with a dodgy leg. Each night for verisimilitude an old fashioned stick telephone, the type with a mouthpiece and a separate ear-piece on the side, is placed squarely in the middle of the table. It too must have survived the siege as it has obviously suffered a major accident at some stage and sits at an alarming angle. The phone has a wire which is always left wrapped around it, nobody seeming to worry much about unwinding it. Martin usually sits at the desk as we wait for the scene to start and each night after unwinding the wire and leading it carefully over the edge of the desk he makes a phone call to his wife, or his bookmaker, or his barber. If only the audience knew what they were missing. After this bit of business Martin moves to the front of the stage where he has decided there is a fourth wall with a large classical painting on it which he lovingly admires, pointing out the Rubenesque cherubs to me in which I show intense interest. A truly magical theatrical moment.

I finally received my cheque last night. Tonight could be the last show we are told.

Sunday, 5 June 2005

It is now unbearably hot during the day, as high as 46°. In the evening it is a little cooler but still well up in the thirties. In order to keep the audience cool fans have been erected around the edge of the seating platform which spray water in a fine mist over the audience. Bearing in mind that the water comes straight from the local water supply I am not at all sure that sitting in the audience is a particularly healthy place to be. Suzie came to see the show last night and if she escapes without contracting something serious it will be a cause for joy.

When I arrived in the green room Meena seemed to be rather upset, in fact I thought she had been crying. I also found Martin deep in thought which seemed a bit odd at the time but I thought no more of it.

It was a night for the army but sponsored by *Hero Honda*. Throughout the site there were soldiers with guns presumably providing security for the head of the army who was attending. He arrived late, no surprise there, and everyone was kept waiting in the melting heat. I was giving a good impression of a self-basting actor when mercifully with the words: *"Long years ago ..."* the show finally began some 50 minutes late, a record.

The show itself was uneventful, indeed a good performance, but the poor audience were kept at the end for a further 20 minutes to hear speeches from the great and the good of *Hero Honda.*

Suzie enjoyed the show, particularly the court and prison scenes.

I later learnt that Aamir had earlier reduced Meena to tears, a scene which Martin had witnessed, and when I had found him deep in thought he was wondering exactly what to do about it.

The usual wait to go home. This time a record, nearly an hour. We eventually arrived back at the hotel at about 12:15 and had a light supper. In the night I was desperately ill and spent much of the small hours in the loo, and all I'd had was the pasta. Soon it will be all over.

Tonight is the last night. Tomorrow, Suzie and I leave for Mussoorie and Shilma. It is a long drive to our destination, *Carlton's Pleasance*, once owned by the East India Company and described as *'a place of peace on the Mussoorie hillside'.* I can't wait.

Monday, 6th June 2005

Last night was the final performance. And I have to say it brought a great sense of release. This has been a marathon commitment in many ways and I confess I am relieved it is finally over.

The final show itself was uneventful. Martin was mentally already on the plane and we had two close calls at corpsing. His appearance as Lord Ismay was as remarkable as ever. Tie rather askew, shirt looking somewhat rustic (it really was very difficult with the shirts we were provided with to make them look at all respectable), jacket open and sporting a fine wide brown belt to hold up his locally tailored trousers which had a habit of slipping somewhat altogether projecting a rather lived-in kind of a look. I imagine that the Indians in the twenties would have been mightily in awe of such a viceroy. I offered to help straighten things out a bit but I think I was in danger of confusing Martin at that stage with someone who did give a fig.

And suddenly with the last, *"Let them burn in their own hatred,"* it was all over.

Martin wanted a make a sharp exit but I felt we ought to stay and be sociable especially as one of the cast had written a short parody of the play which I recall had Sir Thomas Roe espousing the virtues of port wine and Gandhi wanting everyone to smoke marijuana, which as it turned out was rather ironic.

As my contribution to the after-show party I had brought along a couple of bottles of wine. Once the show was finished, I managed to round up a few glasses in the green room, enough for all the main players and we had a convivial drink. We were then called out in front of the audience for the very first time. I though we were going to have some kind of curtain call. Naturally I could not go on stage glass in hand so I carefully found a place to secrete it. As I did so Aamir who was close by said that he did not allow alcohol on the set. But in fact it turned out not to be a curtain call. It was one of those Indian things where someone very important was speaking and we all just stood there. At one point I was beckoned forward and this very nice gentleman told me that he had met Mountbatten … who was somewhat taller than I. Interesting.

A somewhat short
Mountbatten

After this interlude I retrieved my glass and the wine and
made my way into the reception area where everyone was
gathering. As I did so I bumped into Aamir again.
Naturally he was going to say a few nice words about my
performance and thank me for all my efforts. *"I wish you
had spoken to me. I cannot allow any alcohol here,"* was
what he actually said. I was inwardly seething but replied,
"No problem", reminding myself that the underlying
message of the play was one of tolerance and the
consequences of the lack of it.

After that I felt the planned sketch was perhaps no
longer appropriate and as my part was mainly about
espousing the virtues of drink I felt it was unlikely to be
received too well. So after saying a few brief farewells I
prepared to leave. As I did so I met Meena. She had
worked almost every day for two months from eleven in
the morning to almost midnight and in addition had
silently put up with all of Aamir's nonsense probably
earning precious little for her pains. I thanked her for all
she had done telling her that I thought she had done an
amazing job and that if she were my daughter I would be
mightily proud of her. A few moments later she came up
to me in floods of tears and said it was the nicest thing
anyone had said to her. I gave her a big hug and with that
Martin and I wandered off into the night.

We hailed a police car and the sergeant-in-charge amazingly agreed to take us to a place where we could catch a cycle-rickshaw. The rickshaw operators were all asleep on a carpet and the police tried to stir them but to no avail. We thanked the police for their efforts and managed to hail an auto-rickshaw which took us back to the hotel.

After a brief farewell Martin headed for his room. Somehow despite all this madness we had managed to get each other through. Martin had been a good chum over the past two months and outwardly at least had coped a lot better than I. Today Martin heads for home and Suzie and I for the hills.

Clearly I am, despite my very best of intentions, not entirely suited to the Indian way of doing things. Some find it quaint but it just drove me to distraction. Much as I love both India and its people who in the main I found to be warm and loving, it would have to a very special piece of work or an exceptional director to attract me here again. And that's the only reason why any actor should want to work anywhere. If one just wants to see India, my advice is take a holiday.

A FEW CLOSING THOUGHTS

A few thoughts for actors who might contemplate working in India:

-   Read the script. In my case I only saw snippets of the script and came out largely on trust. In hindsight very unwise. It subsequently transpired that the first act and part of the second had obviously been cobbled together from a previous script with the remainder of the second act being largely based on dialogue taken directly from published histories and biographies. At least half of the show was in Hindi. I have never seen a translation but from snippets picked up I suspect it didn't entirely paint a particularly kind picture of the British. But for all that the show appeared to be entertaining and the audience seemed to enjoy it. So first, insist on reading the script and satisfy yourself that it is something you want to do.
-   Check out the director, independently. In my case the two co-directors had impressive CV's but *The Times of India* later described the principal director as: *"...having exchanged theatre for spectacle"*, which I think was fair comment.
-   Check out the other principal actors. What experience do they have?
-   Before committing agree and copy back the terms of engagement in writing since there is unlikely to be any formal agreement. The important matters are the usual sort of things you'd find in any normal agreement :
    o   Dates
    o   Accommodation
    o   Meals and drinks
    o   Flights
    o   Local transport

- o A reasonable weekly payment coupled with an agreed payment schedule. We received Rs8,000 a week. This really was not enough and much of it went on taxi fares.

- Although Indians seem to be offended by putting things in writing, in truth I suspect that it is simply that they don't want to be pinned down because they may be promising things that they know they cannot yet for certain provide. But without some kind of written agreement there is a risk that they will later adjust their version of what has passed between you to suit the present reality.
- Let go of western values – especially in theatre. Remember there is no such thing at the moment as professional theatre in India although this is changing.
- Expect everything to be extremely late and lots of things not to work. The management will be chaotic, the detailed planning non-existent, the timetabling unrealistic, timekeeping and a sense of urgency completely lacking, all causing everything to change, often, and without notice.
- Don't expect much time off and don't make any personal plans.
- Allow huge amounts of extra time for everything you do.
- Always ask open questions (and preferably of more than one person) otherwise the answer will always be 'Yes' which could well mean 'No'. Few people admit to not understanding you.
- Expect power cuts.
- Look after your own corner. Rely on others as little as possible otherwise you will be disappointed.
- And finally, don't waste energy fighting it all. You will change nothing and wear yourself out. Be patient and polite and be prepared to put up with it. Losing your cool will probably result in the very person you're depending on disappearing!

KEEPING HEALTHY

A few pieces of advice based on Ros's advice to me and my own experience:

- Make sure you have all the necessary jabs. Don't be tempted to leave without them.
- Don't forget to take your malaria pills. Last year 200 people returning to England contracted malaria and the vast majority had not taken their pills.
- Keep bites and cuts clean and dry. Use antihistamine cream for angry bites.
- Don't go anywhere near the wild dogs. There are lots of them.
- Keep your nails short and wash your hands often (certainly before every meal) using a nail brush and an antiseptic like Dettol since spores collect behind the fingernails.
- No matter how tempting avoid anything uncooked, especially salads.
- Always peel fruit.
- Don't eat fish unless you're near the sea.
- Don't drink the local water – ever! Only drink bottled water and don't accept bottles where the seal is already broken. And always brush your teeth in bottled water.
- Never take ice in drinks.
- Despite all precautions you will almost certainly get some kind of gut infection. Take advice before you leave and take appropriate medication with you.
- Carry a loo roll – not usually to be found in loos outside the hotel! You're likely to need it!
- Stay in the shade and walk slow!

Lightning Source UK Ltd.
Milton Keynes UK
UKHW020750290819
348791UK00006B/120/P